AUTISM SPECTRUM DISORDER WOMEN IN RELATIONSHIPS

How to understand and Live with an Autism Spectrum Female Partner.

Dr Gina Slater

Table of Content

Part 1

AUTISM SPECTRUM IN WOMEN

Understanding Autism
The neurobehavioral characteristics of a person are impacted by autism. It is known that individuals with autism tend to have high sensory sensitivity, which alters how they perceive their environment. It alters how the brain receives information from the senses and may cause confusion. Compared to someone who does not have the disease, their vision of the world could feel overwhelming.

As a result, it may have an impact on how they communicate and interact with others, making connections and interactions more challenging. For someone with autism, routine settings that are typically thought of as comfortable can feel overpowering. This may also imply that some autistic individuals regard tasks that other people find challenging to be relatively simple.

It is generally accepted that autistic symptoms appear by the age of three. It could take a youngster until they are a year and a half old before communication problems are visible. Sometimes, nevertheless, symptoms are present from birth.

Others might not experience autistic symptoms until a shift in their environment later in life. This is because the new situation is outside of their scope and has never been investigated before. An autistic individual frequently lives their entire life without receiving a diagnosis.

According to the website of the National Autistic Society, women in particular frequently go misdiagnosed for a variety of reasons. In contrast to female qualities, "autism diagnosis tools" are frequently based on male traits, hence while being considered for a diagnosis, they do not meet the profile associated with autism. Additionally, it has been hypothesized that women, more so than males, tend to their problems, which makes them frequently go untreated.

However, with a greater knowledge of the disorder, the number of adult diagnoses is rising, much like a diagnosis in a child.

Autism symptoms include difficulties communicating, especially when discussing emotions, interacting with others, and playing with other kids. Repeated words, gestures, sentences, questions, and food items are further warning signs. Contrary to your expectations, people often use repetitive movements to cope with stress, such as rocking, pacing, and hand motions. Another characteristic linked to autism is an attachment to specific objects. Autism-related people frequently fail to notice other people or outside events.

Children with autism may develop seizures in more severe situations, which may start in adolescence.

Autism sufferers have heightened senses, which may be overpowering, unpleasant, and even painful for them. This has been addressed before. Because the source of their distress may not be apparent, it may be confusing to others around them. Autism sufferers may not react well to change, therefore a change in routine may be highly upsetting for them.

Sometimes, this degree of suffering might lead to self-destructive behaviors. Moreover, depending on the severity of the autism, the development of communication skills may be hampered. They may, however, excel in some academic areas, such as music, art, arithmetic, and memory, where their talents may skyrocket. According to the National Autistic Society, barely one in six individuals with autism hold a job, which shows that many autistic persons struggle with independence and responsibility as adults. Support should help make this aim more attainable, albeit it may not always be a realistic result.

It is well known that an early diagnosis of autism is very advantageous. First of all, it makes people aware of their circumstances and explains why certain behaviors may arise for themselves, their families, friends, and other connections. These folks in the area must take the time to comprehend the implications of autism. According to statistics, 34% of children with ASD believe that bullying is the worst aspect of attending school. This tragic statistic shows how someone's life may be drastically changed with the right assistance and compassion, particularly for children.

How Autism Affects Relationships

Because autistic persons have trouble expressing their feelings, they may find it challenging to negotiate relationships. Even if persons with autism experience emotions, they may be stronger than those experienced by neurotypical people. Autism sufferers are sometimes mistaken for being indifferent because they struggle to communicate their feelings in the manner that is required of them by society.

People with autism can express their emotions improperly because they may struggle to grasp social norms, the way others speak, or body language. These include sentiments of attraction and romance. Clear explanations of what is proper and what is not are necessary for those on the autism spectrum.

For instance, a person with autism could persist in extending an invitation to someone even after they have politely declined many times. This may be the case when the other person declined the offer instead of simply stating "No thanks," using a justification like "I'm busy this weekend."

Because they believe that the other person could still want to go on a date with them, just at a different time, the person with autism is perplexed.

It is suggested that the autistic person refrains from approaching them again if they have once asked them out on a date and they have declined. The autistic person won't re-invite them if they have twice made an excuse.

Relationships and Emotional Dysregulation
Relationships with other people may cause emotional dysregulation in people with autism. "An emotional response that is poorly managed and does not fit within the commonly acknowledged spectrum of emotional reaction" is how emotional dysregulation is defined.

When a spouse acts impulsively and makes snap judgments, such as abruptly taking time away from the other person when upset rather than discussing the matter, this may hurt a relationship.

When a couple often misunderstands each other and finds it difficult to get beyond such misunderstandings, that is another instance of how emotional dysregulation may disrupt relationships. For instance, people fear that the remainder of the dinner will be stressful and unpleasant if there is a conflict at the start of it.

Can 'High-Functioning Autism' Patients Have Romantic Relationships?
A person with autism who can talk, read, write, and execute everyday tasks like dressing and eating is referred to as having high-functioning autism (HFA). HFA patients may live freely.

For the following reasons, some individuals dislike the phrase "high-functioning autism"

When someone has been diagnosed with autism, intelligence is not a reliable indicator of functioning capabilities.

In diagnostic manuals, it is no longer a recognized diagnostic word.

The word is misleading since it makes certain assumptions about people that may not be true.

A person may not have enough functional skills for their age just because they possess standard or anticipated intellectual talents.

The phrase is also archaic.

Although someone with HFA can be in romantic relationships, introvert stereotypes may apply to them. If HFA is understood in this manner, too much engagement with the outside world may be overwhelming for those who have it.

Whether or not they have autism, people in relationships are urged to be patient with those who have HFA. Choosing a restaurant for a date may be challenging for a person with HFA. Both individuals in a relationship must make sure they are consistently in sync. They need to talk about how quickly or slowly they want their relationship to develop.

According to research and clinical observation, the majority of those with HFA are interested in dating. However, there is surprisingly little study on this element of autism spectrum illnesses or methods to promote happy relationships.

People with HFA may use these talents to establish a successful love relationship since they have spent a lot of time honing their interpersonal skills with family and friends.

What Effect Does Autism Have on Sexual Intimacy?
Sharing one's physical, mental, and emotional selves with another person is what intimacy is all about. The spontaneity and fun of sexual interaction may be restricted by the rigidity and demand for

repetition that are common in people with autism. For those with autism, sensitivity to physical touch may sometimes be stressful. The failure to interpret one's partner's thoughts, emotions, or reported sensations may result in misunderstandings, unpleasant experiences—either physical or emotional—as well as shame and guilt.

The same as everyone else, people with autism have a desire for connection and close relationships. However, compared to their neurotypical classmates, individuals with autism may take longer to self-identify these demands. Through their sexual knowledge, convictions, and values, individuals with autism may also express these demands in various ways. For those with impairments, especially those who have autism, comprehending implicit dating conventions and the hierarchy of sex intimacy may prove to be a challenge. Attending focus groups has helped people with autism better comprehend the closeness of romantic relationships.

People with autism have many alternatives when it comes to romantic relationships. These people include those who are already in a relationship or are married, as well as those who live alone, with one person or many others, or by themselves.

Relationship advise for those who are dating autistic people.
Encourage the autistic person to concentrate on their forehead or nose if keeping eye contact is difficult for them.
Open-ended queries are appropriate, such as "What are your plans for the weekend?"
On a date, offer to pay for your date's drink.
Allow your prospective spouse to approach you when they're prepared.
Find mutual interests by starting a casual discussion.
As a starting point for a date activity, consider a shared interest.

Exchanging contact details

Check to see if you both want to go on more dates.

Discover the effects of autism spectrum disorder (ASD) on your relationship by learning more about it.

Recognize and discuss your partner's sensory demands and difficulties.

Find ways to relax, whether you do it together or privately.

If you need relationship guidance or help, seek it out from a professional.

What Are the Advantages of Dating an Autism Person?

The following traits that make people with autism advantageous for dating and relationships include:

Being able to express themselves honestly, for example, how they feel about dating.

Asking direct questions such as, "Are you satisfied with this date?"

Being more capable of feeling emotions than those without ASD.

Having a little possibility of betraying their relationship; being faithful.

Observing minute information about their relationship that others might overlook.

Knowing their partner's preferences, such as a favorite brand of a chocolate bar, and bringing them presents that reflect their preferences.

Being very understanding of their lover and possessing a very pure heart.

Having the patience to wait patiently for their spouse to finish their drink.

How to know your Partner has ASD.

She is touch-resistant.

When a person has ASD, they may not be as loving as you'd want and could behave as if you're torturing them when you offer them an unprompted hug. It's not that they can't express their affection; they just need to be at ease and in the correct frame of mind before they can cuddle, embrace, or snuggle.

She is socially awkward

When it comes to social circumstances, persons on the autism spectrum have several difficulties. They could avoid eye contact, converse inappropriately, and struggle to interpret others' gestures, body language, and facial emotions.

Because they struggle with small chats and can't tell when someone is being sarcastic, individuals with ASD may want to avoid social situations as much as possible. I believe that having trouble conversing, for instance, makes it very difficult to forge deep connections with others, whether they be friendships or love relationships. Additionally, we have trouble reading social signs, comprehending other people's views, and predicting how others will truly respond to what we say or do. Building these connections is very tough for persons with autism because of this kind of difficulty.

She has peculiar physical tendencies.
Repetitive speech, bodily tics, and staring anywhere other than a person's eyes while speaking to them are some of the traditional signs of ASD. Due to their challenges adapting to their surroundings, people on the spectrum may display strange behavior.
Unusual tense or focused interests. Stereotyped and repetitive body movements like hand flapping and spinning. Repetitive use of objects like turning lights on and off, insistence on sticking to routines, unusual sensory interests like sniffing objects, and sensory sensitivity issues like avoiding common sounds are just a few examples of behaviors that may be present.

Part 2

WHAT WOMEN LIVING WITH AUTISM
SPECTRUM NEED IN RELATIONSHIPS.

Finding a balance between one's demands
and expectations and those of one's spouse
may be difficult for most relationships.
There are probably a lot more chances for
miscommunication and annoyance in a
relationship if one person is autistic. Every
devoted couple hopes to find a way to a
long-lasting, respectful, loving, and
rewarding relationship.

It has been beneficial that there is now more
knowledge and materials available on
relationships with neuro-diverse people.
There are more options for individuals,
couples, and women dating men with
autism spectrum disorders.

This post is a succinct compilation of data
compiled from my own experience and the

many women who have confided in me over the years. You may find a list of resources after this article to help you find more information on this topic.

1. Become familiar with Autism Spectrum Disorders (and how ASD affects your partner)

Autism is a neurological condition that impairs perception, language, social interaction, learning, and behavior. A person with autism spectrum disorder may quickly become overstimulated by information processed by the senses. On the other side, a person with autism may also struggle to integrate sensory information and exhibit under activity, unresponsiveness, and/or a particular reaction to sensory input.

For someone with autism spectrum disorder, communication is typically received and understood differently. When communicating verbally, words are often taken literally and absorbed more slowly. Autism spectrum individuals often struggle to hold a conversation and remain on topic. The same holds for social skills. Making eye contact may be challenging, and sometimes facial expressions don't accurately convey how someone is feeling. It is common to ignore or misinterpret social signals. Autism spectrum disorder patients are unsure about how to interact with others. Each person's issues come through uniquely. Many people with autism spectrum disorders also experience anxiety.

Most likely, your spouse struggles with executive function. Planning, organizing, prioritizing, time management, emotional control, and impulse control are all examples of executive function activities. For those with autism spectrum disorders, inertia may be difficult, both when beginning and ending activity. This lack of drive, along with other behavioral or psychological issues, maybe incorrectly blamed for these executive function impairments. Many executive function duties are often handled by non-spectrum partners in romantic relationships.

Numerous novels have been produced recently regarding couples when one spouse has autism spectrum disorder. Books authored by experts and by women married to men with autism spectrum disorders are also available. Some of them were authored by couples as well. After this article is a list of some of these novels. It may be quite reassuring to read about other people's experiences and sentiments. Remember that every relationship is different. The novels may be rather depressing. Your spouse who is on the autism spectrum will have his autistic traits as well as a special experience and personality profile, and he may also have other co-occurring conditions that contribute to his uniqueness.

You and/or your spouse may be working on accepting the diagnosis if it is a fresh one. It can be hard for one of you, if not both of you, to accept. You may be lamenting the loss of earlier expectations as you try to understand more about ASD and how it affects your spouse and your relationship.

It would be beneficial to look for competent experts and/or join a support group for women coupled with men on the autism spectrum as you learn more and attempt to acknowledge the role an autistic spectrum condition plays in your relationship. These materials are accessible but could be challenging to locate. Making a list of the admirable traits your spouse has that you find attractive might also be useful. These should be kept in mind at all times, particularly during trying times in a partnership.

Additionally, keeping a list of your strengths will be beneficial. When you are going through really challenging and perplexing circumstances, it might be tough to recall these great aspects of oneself. Your self-esteem will be raised and you'll be more motivated as you navigate the difficulties in your relationship if you keep in mind all the good things about both you and your spouse. I have come to admire the partners with ASD and non-spectrum disorders' commitment to finding solutions to forge a more solid and loving relationship throughout the years.

Identify and attend to sensory needs (and issues with your partner)
Persons with autism spectrum disorders often struggle with sensory difficulties. One or more of the senses may be impacted, as was previously described. Senses can be either under or overexposed (hyposensitive). Some ASD sufferers are overly sensitive to different illumination. For instance, they see the flickering of fluorescent lights and/or hear its buzzing.

Some people have headache triggers. A person with autism may have excessive sensitivity to certain environmental noises and/or scents. Even while true pinpricks may not be felt at all, light touches may simulate them.

A person with autism spectrum disorder may seem in certain circumstances to be unable to interpret sensory data from one or more of the usual five senses of sight, hearing, taste, and touch. They may seem to miss things that are right in front of them or interpret speech as "noise." These circumstances might seem to be exceedingly odd. For many people on the autism spectrum, three more lesser-known sensory systems are often impacted as well. There are three systems: the interoceptive system, the proprioceptive system, and the vestibular system. The proprioceptive system is responsible for balance (state of internal body functions). The eighth sense is often used to describe interoception.

There is some evidence that people with autism spectrum disorders might have both improved and impaired self-perception. Atypical interoception or interceptive dysfunction refers to this. Several people have reported having little awareness of the need to eat, drink, or go to the restroom (due to hunger). Some women claim that they often have to remind their partners to eat or drink, particularly when they are completely absorbed in something else.

The choice of clothing, food, bedding, and furniture that are comfortable for both couples as well as what kinds of places and activities may be pleasurable for both partners are just a few examples of how sensory disorders may affect almost every area of life. Higher levels of sensory processing may be advantageous in some circumstances, such as when it comes to processing visual data fast or in unusual ways. Because they have strong visual processing abilities, people with autism, like your spouse, may be skilled in designing, building, and engineering.

Sensory requirements or problems might alter over time or even day to day. Your spouse has probably developed coping mechanisms to deal with or avoid different types of environmental sensory input as an adult. Tinted glasses, earphones, caps, or certain clothing choices are some popular tactics used to successfully reduce ambient sensory overload. Some people like to have little "fidgets" about the house because they may be relaxing and assist with sensory overload.

Some people may find it beneficial to use a weighted blanket and sleep in complete darkness at home. Hopefully, it is simpler to manage illumination, as well as the environment's noises and odors, at home. It might sometimes be advantageous to work with an occupational therapist who has received sensory integration training.

Intimacy may also be affected by sensory difficulties. With improved comprehension, patience, and the development of solutions to meet the requirements of both partners, sensory concerns in the bedroom may be resolved. You and your companion may talk about different sensory preferences and think about practical modifications.

When under stress, a person on the autism spectrum is more likely to feel sensory overload and, as a consequence, to shut down or maybe even have a "meltdown." Adults on the autistic spectrum who are self-aware are often able to see early warning indicators and create escape and calming techniques. When both partners are aware of this, they may cooperate to find a solution that works for everyone. When one spouse has an ASD and wants to take a break or is getting overstimulated, many couples learn signs to express this. There are many different types of breaks that may be negotiated beforehand. This can include bringing two automobiles to an event, if necessary so that the ASD partner can leave and the non-ASD spouse won't have to.

Discover and Apply Communication Techniques (that work best for you and your partner)
Communication at its best is crucial in any relationship but it is a weakness for someone with ASD. It may be extremely challenging to decipher non-verbal communication, such as facial expressions, gestures, and voice intonation. Initiating verbal communication may be challenging for those with autism. These issues are not a result of a lack of drive, but rather of a difference in neurobiology.

Your spouse will benefit from your straightforward, calm, and consistent communication. Once the person with ASD knows how to satisfy their partner's needs, they often desire to do so. It's critical to express your social, emotional, mental, physical, and sexual requirements clearly. Partners should talk about information about behavioral expectations together. Instead of thinking about correction, consider explanation. Share your expectations with your spouse, and then ask him to share his.

You will often need to give your spouse clear, detailed directions that they can follow. For instance, if you require your partner's assistance with a task like doing the laundry, make sure to provide detailed instructions on what, when, and how the garments should be done. It may be necessary to have a system in place for organizing laundry baskets if your spouse is unable to decide what to wash. For instance, square baskets may be used for clean laundry while circular baskets can be utilized for filthy clothes.

Your spouse with autism may need specific instruction and practice in hugging techniques. Remember not to interpret your partner's behaviors and wants through your non-spectrum lens even if it may seem that he or she does not want to be affectionate with you. It's crucial to go over any areas of need in-depth. Many facets of life will need extremely direct and precise communication. Texting, emailing, and/or writing down information on paper, sticky notes, calendars, or wipe-off boards may all be extremely helpful to certain couples.

Consider setting aside some time each day to converse and sit down. For optimum communication, it can be ideal to sit next to one another. Nearly all people with ASD report finding it challenging to comprehend spoken information while keeping eye contact. This would be particularly valid while talking about each other's needs. This time spent together may significantly improve life satisfaction and strengthen your relationship.

Once again, think about utilizing visual material to express or support spoken communications (notes, emails, a whiteboard, even illustrations from books or other visual media). Be innovative. When our partners on the autism spectrum are having difficulties due to anxiety, sensory overload, or executive functioning issues, visual information may be utilized as a permanent resource since it is considerably simpler for most autistic people to assimilate.

Be aware that you may not fully comprehend your partner's viewpoint. To be more precise. Recognize that your spouse could find it difficult to clarify a situation or even to realize that explanation is required. Non-spectrum partners cannot presume that they comprehend the significance of a certain behavior shown by their ASD spouse by using their non-spectrum filter for ASD behavior. The autism-spectrum spouse could also struggle to comprehend their requirements. Each couple should determine their requirements and communicate them to the other. If you have to explain to your spouse every action you take to satisfy your wants, it can not sound sincere. Though it may be challenging at first, do not interpret this as an indication that your spouse doesn't care. Consider it a crucial step in increasing our mutual understanding, trust, and respect.

Discover Outlets to Relax (together and individually)

Your spouse and you probably use different strategies to reduce stress. Everyone is unique, and everyone relaxes differently. You may encounter greater differences in a neuro-diverse partnership, which may initially test you both. You both must develop your coping mechanisms and communicate your requirements to one another. To relieve stress and tension, partners must respect one another's needs and strategies. This may sometimes imply distinct or "parallel" activity. The spouse who is autistic may want a lot of alone time or "extra" time to pursue their hobbies.

For your spouse who is on the autistic spectrum, going from work to home could be difficult. Men on the autistic spectrum often report a first "alone break" after getting home as "important." Without understanding and properly preparing for this crucial transition break, a relationship barrier may occur.

It may be incredibly irritating to have to put off connecting and communicating with your spouse. To express their stress levels at this time of day, couples may utilize a visual approach, such as a wipe-off board. When your boyfriend first arrives home, prepare for his time by himself. Set aside 30 minutes or whatever is practical and fair for you. After that, you may arrange some time with each other or the kids. Later in the evening, extra alone time might be planned, if necessary. It is possible to plan jobs and activities in addition to chores. Predictable nights may significantly increase the likelihood of more pleasurable and peaceful moments spent together as a pair while also reducing stress.

Having fun together may be a great way to strengthen relationships. Encourage laughter in your shared lives. The connection will be improved, and some of the "extra" tension will be reduced. If you can find the proper things to do as a couple, it can be amazing. This may include jointly exploring your passions. Initially, this could need more patience, particularly if setting clear limits is crucial. Exploring concurrent activities is another option. Although you are both in the same room or area, you can be doing something else for a while. Choosing the appropriate time frame in advance might be useful. One may set a timer or another specific reminder. Be original!

You will probably be the one organizing the social activities since social gatherings may be challenging for someone with ASD. You could be the one who is most interested in these activities and has the best "neurological" (i.e., executive function) talents to organize things. Your spouse could be agreeing with your plans because he wants to win your approval and/or will find most things more enjoyable if you are there.

Once kids are aware of what to anticipate, they often have fun. If your spouse can be assigned a "role" at different social gatherings, it might be advantageous. Any duty that would benefit the event, such as aiding with setup or verifying the food or drink, may fall under this category. Discuss and make plans for what this entails. Additionally, talk about choices for a private area or location to go to when you need a break from social activities.

When socializing becomes too demanding or interesting, your spouse may want a real "exit" plan. As previously indicated, one strategy couples often use is to drive two vehicles, allowing the ASD partner to depart before his stress levels rise to the point of causing a shutdown or breakdown.

You could have discovered that your spouse is prepared to devote a lot of time to pursue a particular hobby. This is a useful method of relaxation. This time must be balanced with other activities of daily life and time spent as a pair. This time can, if at all feasible, be arranged but is flexible. Your ASD spouse could need more time spent pursuing his hobbies and/or time alone during periods of higher stress.

You may also need to set aside time for your hobbies. If this entails more socializing, you may want to consider making plans with friends, joining groups, volunteering, or engaging in other activities that involve others. In addition to receiving emotional fulfillment from your spouse, you can discover that you also require these extracurricular activities and social occasions to interact with others.

Find Expert Assistance (for ASD and any secondary mental health needs)

Finding expert assistance for the communication and sensory problems you have as a couple may be crucial and required. Talking to a specialist about executive function problems might also be beneficial. As was previously indicated, someone on the autistic spectrum may have extremely poor executive function abilities. Finding a specialist who can deal with problems with executive function may be challenging, but the effort is worthwhile.

Those who have an autistic spectrum condition should be informed that they are more likely to have depression, anxiety, obsessive-compulsive disorder, and/or other mental health illnesses. Negative social interactions and experiences that result in low self-esteem may also have an impact on your partner's mental health.

You could also struggle with your mental health. At some point in their lives, around 40% of the general population will fulfill the requirements for a mental health diagnosis. It is estimated that at least 69 percent of persons on the autism spectrum have co-occurring mental health problems. As a result of your connection with your spouse, you may also be more likely to feel anxiety and/or depression, particularly if he has just received a diagnosis and/or treatment.

ASD sufferers can need regular intervals of social seclusion. It could be difficult to accept this without taking it personally. In part as a coping technique and due to his inability to figure out how to make you happy, your spouse may have also established a tendency of withdrawing to his specific hobbies. He could not have the information necessary to carry out your intentions as a result of communication gaps and problems. He eventually concludes that it is better to do nothing than the incorrect thing.

Misunderstandings and issues will arise as time goes on while living together in a house. You could experience a lack of communication and emotional connection with your spouse as a result of the nature of ASD. It's possible that while you strive to fix your relationship, your contact with other people will become more restricted, which will make you feel even more alone. Depression and sometimes even emotions of hopelessness might result from this. It may be crucial for you and your spouse to get evaluated and treated for any mental health issues for several reasons.

Dealing with a professional who is knowledgeable about and experienced in working with individuals on the autism spectrum is crucial. You should look for a therapist who has an interest in fostering neuro-diverse interactions and who has characteristics that are compatible with someone who has autism if one who is knowledgeable and experienced regarding ASD is not readily accessible.

Women with autism often discuss their need for direct communication from their partners while talking about dating. They complain, "I just wish they would explain what they mean." Even though many autistic women have a tremendous ability for love and empathy, social cues may nevertheless elude them. Indirect communication and sarcasm are ultimately what may make a relationship very difficult and unpleasant for a woman with autism.

Additionally, their partners could feel uncomfortable due to their demand for direct communication. Teens and adults with autism often speak their minds. They may be so blunt that this unnerves neurotypicals. For instance, a lady with autism may just state, "I don't want to hang out with you," if she wants to spend time with her particular interest and recharge her social batteries. If her spouse doesn't get her need for alone time, this phrase might be quite hurtful.

Women who have neurodiversity are more likely to be abused or assaulted.
Unwanted sexual approaches or other manipulative indicators may go unnoticed due to their requirement for direct indications. This could make many women with autism vulnerable to exploitation by their spouses. In fact, according to recent research, autistic women are far more likely to experience abuse since they prefer direct communication, don't grasp social conventions like flirtation, and lack basic sexual knowledge.

Women on the autistic spectrum who date sometimes adopt strong stances in their relationships.

In their relationships, autistic women typically end up taking care of others.

Many women on the autistic spectrum find it difficult to date because they wind up taking care of a spouse who is too dependent. Women with high-functioning autism tend to date men who have a range of mental or physical health issues, in my experience. This implies that they stop taking care of their own needs and instead become obsessed with supporting their lover.

Autistic women have incredible research abilities, so they may read everything they can to support their spouses. Unfortunately, they may become victims to partners who take advantage of their propensity for providing care and their slavish devotion to them. For instance, some autistic women support a needy spouse financially because they love them so much.

On the other side, a woman with autism may get overwhelmed by the idea that women in general—autistic or not—should take on the duty of caretaker. Many autistic women need alone time to concentrate on their unique hobbies or to refuel their social batteries. Their spouse could get estranged from them due to their desire for alone time and begin to feel unwanted or unloved. And this might provide serious difficulties in a love relationship.

Women with autism may use their relationship as a barrier to the outside world.
Being autistic may cause sensory overload and social interaction fatigue. Some autistic women want a spouse who can provide protection and handle errands like grocery shopping and making phone calls to pay the bills. For a woman with autism, working and

doing these errands may be tremendously stressful. She has a natural apprehension about chatting on the phone, so it can take her the whole day to get up the nerve to call. What may seem like a simple chore to others may prove to be quite difficult for someone on the spectrum. Unfortunately, many autistic women lack the lifelong resources they need to help them cope with their overwhelming emotions and the social environment. To protect themselves from the outside world, they could take sanctuary in their connection.

When their relationship is their particular focus, women with autism often make their spouses uncomfortable.

Last but not least, a lot of women with autism struggle with developing strong attachments to their partners. They may even believe that their partner serves as an anchor for them, helping them to cope with their stress, anxiety, or sensory overload. Sometimes their partner develops into their area of interest. They can also be preoccupied with their union. When something doesn't fit with their ideal relationship, they frequently become upset. If the other person feels uncomfortable with the level of attention their partner is giving them, this could ultimately lead to the breakdown of a relationship.

Understanding oneself is crucial for autistic spectrum individuals who want to date.
Learning more about yourself and how you operate in a relationship is crucial if you're a woman with ASD who struggles with dating others on the autistic spectrum. It will assist you in pinpointing any weaknesses you may have, your strengths as a partner, and the characteristics of your ideal partnership. You may use this to discover a companion who supports you and your special requirements.

You also need to think about how you want to self-disclose that you have autism and how you want to advocate for yourself to get the support you need. You can better manage your partner's or potential partner's expectations by being open and honest about your neurodiversity. It will lessen misunderstandings and help them better understand your needs.

Understanding Yourself Before Dating
Write down your responses to the following questions once you have a moment:

What are your sensitivity levels to sound, touch, smell, taste, and vision?
What does sensory overload feel like on the inside?
What bodily feelings are you experiencing?
How does it affect your disposition?
What effect does it have on your capacity to listen, think, and speak?
How can you and your spouse lessen your sensory overstimulation?
What is the state of your social battery?

What kind of social situations make you feel worn out?

What must you do to refresh yourself?

Which routine duties stress you out?

With your spouse, discuss these responses. Have many chats about it since they may not share your sensations and may find it difficult to comprehend at first. It's crucial to talk about your wants and how your spouse can fulfill them.

Relationships do need giving and receiving. You and your spouse may opt to attend a party together since it has a special meaning for them. The importance of the events for both you and your spouse must be considered. Additionally, you may need to make a concession, such as agreeing to stay at the party for only two hours before leaving for home.

Online autism treatment is beneficial. Even if you already have a relationship, self-awareness is still necessary. Think for a minute about how you want your relationship to be and what qualities you are seeking in a mate. Additionally, it could be time to think about autism treatment or autism group therapy if you're having problems with your spouse or notice that you can't think about much else but them. Through autism treatment, you may pick up new coping mechanisms for emotional discomfort, sensory overload, and anxiety, as well as social skills and advocacy techniques.

Part 3

THE DIFFERENCE BETWEEN YOU AND HER

Men are seen as the norm in many spheres of life, including healthcare, and women suffer as a consequence since it is believed that female bodies operate similarly. We are aware that some illnesses, including heart attacks and strokes, manifest differently in women than they do in males, and this knowledge gap may have disastrous effects on women.

Similar to other developmental disorders, autism or autism spectrum disorder (ASD) manifests differently in women (by "women" we mean everyone born female) than it does in males, according to several studies. There is sadly a severe paucity of scientific study in this area, as there are many women's difficulties. To help you recognize the indicators of autism in yourself or others, we believe it's crucial to summarize what is known about autism in females. We recommend additional studies on everything we will briefly touch on in this introductory essay since this is a highly deep and complicated issue.

Let's start by going through some typical autistic symptoms in adults:
finding it difficult to comprehend what others are experiencing or thinking

Being very apprehensive in social settings.

finding it difficult to establish acquaintances or favor solitude.

Seeming without intention to be harsh, unpleasant, or uninterested in others.

Having difficulty expressing your feelings.

Interpreting things extremely literally, for instance, you may not see the humor in expressions like "break a leg".

Having a daily routine and being very worried if it varies.

What do we know about female autism?

Although statistics differ, it is generally acknowledged that males are diagnosed with autism more often than women. According to current statistics, three males are diagnosed with autism for every woman.

There might be several causes for this, however. Overall, research indicates that it is doubtful that ASD occurs equally often in men and women, but mounting data indicates that the prevalence rates may vary even more across the sexes because of the way that ASD present in women. Numbers and statistics may also be affected by the fact that women tend to get clinical ASD diagnoses at much later ages and with long delays between first examination and diagnosis.

What symptoms of ASD do women have?
Even while each girl and woman with ASD is different, many have similar experiences. The Asperger/Autism Network states that a girl with ASD might:

Recognize her differences by noting how her interests vary from those of her classmates.

like playing alone or with only one or two partners, while appreciating and concentrating on certain hobbies

Aversion to what is in style, popular, or feminine should be evident.

She may be sensitive to textures and prefer to wear relaxed, functional attire.

due to her lack of familiarity with current trends or social mores, come off as naïve or immature.

Work hard to "camouflage" her social apprehension or uncertainty via tactful mimicry, daydream or nature escapes, or iding social interaction.

Display many facets of her personality in various contexts.

be more prone to have meltdowns at home to let out her pent-up feelings.

be worn out from the effort of figuring out social norms or from copying others around her to conceal her deviations.

Be fearful in circumstances when she is expected to perform in front of others. This could result in mutism, escapism, or an emphasis on rituals and routines.

Problems with identifying ASD in women: Since there are no accurate biomarkers for autism, the disorder is diagnosed primarily on observation and description of the core traits that significantly interfere with daily functioning. The fact that the behavioral indicators utilized as diagnostic criteria were chosen based on preconceived notions of what autistic behaviors should look like is a fundamental problem with the present diagnosis process. These standards were created using the mostly male populations that had previously been classified as autistic. However, further research on the traits and their effects on people of all ages and genders is required. Evidence would imply that it is underdiagnosed in women because they show their autism in ways that do not fit these current diagnostic criteria.

When addressing this subject, the female autism phenotype (FAP) and the idea of camouflaging (compensating for and disguising autistic features), in particular, often come up.

The theory of camouflaging in autistic women contends that women can conceal socio-communication. Impairments due to increased sensitivity to social pressure to fit in, gendered expectations for social behavior, and strengths in some social-communication skills, have been supported by differences in the manifestation of autistic traits in these individuals. This is especially prevalent in girls who fall into the high-functioning category of autism.

Making eye contact with people during talks is a common way of camouflaging.

Prepare your jokes or conversational phrases in advance.

imitating other people's social behavior

mimicking motions and facial expressions

Autism symptoms may be hidden by both males and females, although it seems to affect girls and women more often. This may help to explain why women are less likely to get an autism diagnosis.

To get to any definite conclusions on autism in women, much more extensive, long-term research is required since so much is still unknown or speculative. However, we firmly think that it is beneficial to start these conversations about more general concerns, such as how women are treated in healthcare and the potential consequences of this. This discussion makes us aware of the numerous diseases and health problems that vary between men and women, as well as the possible influence that society and our settings may have on some behavioral difficulties.

As was said, there have been significant advancements in the study of autism spectrum disorder, but adult women who believe they may be autistic still have trouble gaining a diagnosis and accessing care. Consult your GP first if you think you may have undiagnosed autism. It can take a few medical visits before you discover one who can relate to your symptoms and worries. You may assess your symptoms and rule out other reasons with the aid of a psychologist.

Benefits of Being with an Autistic Partner.

There are many fantastic advantages to dating an autistic person, but there may also be a little learning curve.

There are numerous myths regarding autism, with some of the more prevalent focusings on autistic individuals and sexual relationships.

Some people think that those with autism aren't attracted to or incapable of romantic love. But this couldn't be farther from the truth.

In actuality, partners with autism may be fantastic. There are numerous benefits to dating an autistic person that is seldom discussed, albeit you may need to be patient while teaching social signs and conventions to your spouse.

Can someone with autism date?
Yes! Many autistic persons are more than capable of dating, having physical intimacy, and empathizing with their relationships, albeit not necessarily all autistic people.

When it comes to dating, autistic individuals often encounter a special set of difficulties, but that doesn't mean they can't have happy, fulfilling relationships.

Dating success and experience
According to a 2016 study by trusted Sources, 73 percent of high-functioning autistic respondents reported having romantic relationships. In actuality, just 7% of interviewees said they had no interest in

dating. The research also discovered that autistic couples reported more relationship satisfaction than autistic-neurotypical couples.

Similar to this, a 2017 research found that, regardless of who they are dating, the majority (74 percent) of autistic persons are content in their relationships. Only 9% of participants said they were unhappy with their relationship. 29 percent of the autistic singles polled expressed remorse about their single status.

Autistic persons are more likely to be single than neurotypical people, even though research has generally refuted the assumption that they are less likely to be interested in romantic relationships.

For instance, a 2017 study indicated that just 50% of individuals who were autistic were in partnerships, compared to 70% of neurotypical people.

A 2019 research also showed that relationships with autistic persons often terminate sooner. Compared to neurotypical people, they worry more about their future relationships, especially how to meet potential love partners.

The advantages of perhaps dating an autistic person
Only 20% of participants in a 2016 study trusted Source acknowledged being in a relationship with an autistic person, suggesting that autistic persons more often date neurotypical people.

There are numerous benefits to being in a relationship with someone who is autistic, even though neurotypical individuals may need to change while dating an autistic person.

These advantages might include:

Honesty.

People with autism are often seen as being highly honest. Although it might sometimes seem a little "brutal," this degree of honesty offers advantages. Knowing that your spouse is being genuine with you and saying what they mean, particularly when they are complimenting you, may increase your sense of confidence. If you are accustomed to dating individuals who tend to downplay their beliefs or shy away from disagreement, this could be a welcome change of pace.

Reliability.
Relationships with autistic persons often seem secure and steady because they appreciate regularity and order. You could have fewer shocks and more regularity in your life.

Loyalty.
If you're seeking a committed partner, you could get along well with someone who has autism. According to 2010 research, autistic persons are often far more interested in

long-term relationships than they are in short-term hookups. With the popularity of dating apps and the hookup culture, autism may be a welcome change of pace for friendship.

Things to remember
Every relationship has its own special set of difficulties that often need some adaptation. When dating an autistic individual, the same holds. Although each individual is unique, certain typical difficulties arise when dating an autistic person.

Interpreting social signals
Autism often manifests as difficulty interpreting social dynamics and signals, such as:

Sarcastic body language and tone
flirting\eye-rolling
hostile statements

When dating an autistic individual, it's usually essential to be as clear-cut as you can to prevent misunderstandings. If you're outraged or offended by anything your spouse said, it could be preferable to express how what they did hurt you as precisely as you can rather than assuming they can know you're upset and why.

Additionally, you may need to be a bit more direct than usual while expressing your love interest at the beginning of the relationship. Some autistic individuals have a harder problem interpreting social signals, such as whether it's appropriate to lean in for a kiss or ask someone out on a date.

Adhering to societal standards
Similar to this, understanding social norms and conventions in many contexts might be difficult for someone with autism. If your spouse doesn't automatically know how to act on a date or while meeting your friends

and family for the first time, you will probably need to be understanding.

It doesn't imply that they can't pick up these traditions. Just a bit more direct instruction is needed than for a neurotypical individual. That's OK too.

Additionally, some autistic people believe that "masking"—the practice of concealing one's autism—is required of them. Although there is nothing wrong with trying to learn more about social signals and traditions, it is best to avoid urging your autistic spouse to act differently since masking may have some bad repercussions as well (i.e., forcing them to mask). Be as understanding and accepting of them as you can.

Having too much stimulation
Being easily overstimulated is another defining trait of autism. Feeling overstimulated in big social gatherings or

sensitive to physical contact are two examples of this.

Respecting your partner's limits while having sexual or physical contact is crucial. In actuality, you should adhere to this advice regardless of your romantic relationship.

A dislike of change
Last but not least, individuals with autism often struggle to adjust to change. It may need a bit more preparation and less spontaneity than you're accustomed to having such a connection with someone who has autism.

Your spouse could be accustomed to doing things like eating the same thing every day, going to bed at the same time every night, and putting their things away in the same location every day.

Your spouse could feel a little overburdened if you surprise them with social gatherings. Your spouse may be able to emotionally prepare for changes in their schedule or daily routine with some planning and enough warning.

To make these gatherings seem like a regular part of your partner's week, it could even be helpful to designate certain evenings of the week as "social nights."

Good advice

There may be some advice that might assist you to manage your relationship with an autistic individual, especially in the beginning, even if every relationship is different.

You may wish to bear the following in mind:

When speaking, strive to be as straightforward as you can; give your partner space when they want it (especially after they have been overstimulated)

Be sympathetic if your spouse needs to withdraw from a social situation and learn your partner's preferences for touch early on.

To avoid shocking your spouse with too many changes at once, keep in mind that certain duties can be simpler for you to do than for them, and make the necessary adjustments (e.g., household chore split)

Be considerate of your partner's probable need for regularity and structure.

Let's review.

According to research, neurotypical and autistic individuals have the same desire for romantic relationships. Simply said, they often find it a little harder to understand social signs and handle dating, especially early in a relationship.

The process of discovering what a partner needs to feel comfortable and happy in a relationship is no different from dating a neurotypical person, even if you may need to make certain adaptations when speaking or engaging with an autistic person. Beginnings usually include a learning curve.

And every individual you date has both advantages and disadvantages. For instance, autistic individuals often exhibit these qualities in particular, which are some of the most crucial qualities for a committed partnership. Simply communicate in a directer manner than you are used to, and be ready to give your partner space if they get overstimulated.

In other words, autistic persons can and do experience love and romantic relationships. It can simply seem a bit different than how you're accustomed to it to be in a relationship with an autistic individual.
Relationships and sex may present some difficulties for autistic persons. An autistic

person may, nonetheless, have a satisfying sexual life.

Autism may have an impact on a person's social interactions, learning abilities, behavior, and communication skills.

There is no need for treatment. A person's brain may just function differently from how society expects them to if they are autistic.

Autism is referred to as a spectrum condition since it may have a variety of effects on individuals. Some autistic persons need more assistance than others. This may indicate that they need help with basic responsibilities or abilities like language and conduct.

Other autistic persons may need to require little assistance or none at all.

Having autism often makes it difficult for a person to engage with others. When it comes to developing connections, this could provide some difficulties.

A friend or family member may be able to help autistic person comprehend their sexual sensations if they require assistance. An autistic person has to understand that having sexual desires is completely normal.

An individual may assist a loved one who has autism in realizing that sex is normal and should be joyful. Sexual activities, however, should only be performed by adults with an agreement and are private.

The following advice may be helpful when addressing sexual emotions with an autistic person:

Let them know that it is okay to talk about their feelings and that they are welcome to inquire about sex and sexuality.
Be honest, open, and judgment-free in your communication.
Talk to them about sex education.

Teach them how to discuss their desires and dissatisfactions with a sexual partner.

Talk to them about sexual partners and how to bring up limits.

Tell them that any potential partner should treat them with respect.

How can autism impact a person's sexual development?

An individual may grow sexually even with autism. According to research from 2021, the majority of teens and young adults with autism are interested in relationships and sex.

The research also found that teenagers and young people with autism on average knew less about sex and privacy. This implied that they were more inclined to act inappropriately sexually.

According to researchers, there are many possible causes for this lack of sexual awareness.

difficulty interacting with others
a lack of sexual education and the assumption that persons with autism do not experience sexual attraction
stigmatization
refusal to engage in social activities
on sexual education
Adolescents with autism need adequate sex education, which is vital. They may get knowledge of what is and isn't acceptable in society as a result.

Additionally, sex education may help autistic teenagers be ready for the physical changes that come with puberty.

According to Planned Parenthood, parents and other adults should try to educate their kids about:

Before puberty, as their body starts to grow, reproductive health and methods to lower the chance of pregnancy and STDs
both proper and improper actions

An autistic individual may sometimes struggle to make eye contact. In this situation, talking about these subjects while out on a stroll together or making dinner together could be beneficial.

What if a period starts at school? is one example of a "what if" question that a parent or other caretaker could use in a dialogue to generate answers.

They should also discuss how to respect boundaries and be mindful of any crushes the youngster or teen may have.

How does sex impact autism?

Some autistic individuals may discover that engaging in intimate activities relieves their tension or anxiety, according to the Organization for Autism Research (OAR).

However, certain characteristics of autism may provide difficulties.

heightened sensitivity
Some individuals may experience discomfort due to sensory sensitivity to the

noises and physical sensations of intercourse.

A person should tell their spouse if they are uncomfortable or do not want to do anything. Nobody should feel pressured into doing something they don't want to.

Finding solutions may be made simpler by talking about their requirements with a partner. For instance, individuals may wear light clothing during sex if skin-to-skin contact bothers them or tie their hair up if tickling bothers them.

Communication
Communication is always key when starting a sexual relationship. Before participating in sexual activity, people may benefit from discussing their needs with their partners.

They could benefit from the following advice:

Choose a sound or phrase that is safe to use to signal "stop."
Before engaging in exercise, make a "yes, no, or maybe" list.
Keep a notepad close to the bed so they can refer to it if necessary.
An autistic person might be concerned about telling a potential partner about their autism. They might worry that the other person won't view them favorably. A person with autism should only reveal their diagnosis if they feel at ease doing so.

People would want to break up with a spouse if they see the following:

overlooks the necessity for communication
overlooks the requirements of their senses
attempts to put them in a sour mood
Sex may be overpowering as well. When stressed, autistic persons may have trouble communicating. This could make you feel uneasy or anxious.

During sex, individuals might choose to make "yes" or "no" gestures. People who get too overwhelmed to express themselves verbally during sex might touch their partner on the back to ask for the action to end.

navigating sex's social implications
It might be challenging to recognize verbal or nonverbal signs.
Source they may rely on for certain autistic persons.

It may be advantageous for an autistic person to inform prospective partners that they must be honest with them. As an autistic person may not notice if their spouse is indicating discomfort during sex, this might also be useful.

Talking to the other person when in a sexual relationship is the finest thing a person can do. Things may be more fun if people communicate honestly and freely. It's crucial to understand the distinction between conduct that is appropriate in public and private contexts. It might contribute to everyone's safety.

Stable connections
There are many different kinds of relationships, and they may be tricky to manage. A person's conduct might be suitable or improper depending on the connection.

A mutual, reciprocal emotional and/or sexual connection between two individuals is considered to be a romantic relationship.

According to the OAR, positive relationships have the following qualities:

Communication, emotional and physical decorum, honesty, equality, and mutual acceptance are all virtues.
Dating may be difficult, thus it's important to keep in mind:

It's normal to have crushes, and you may have crushes on several people.

It's OK to not have any crushes.

While flirting may be enjoyable, it's crucial to respect others' limits.

Communication is crucial in relationships since being in one may be difficult.

Even if it is tough, breaking up with someone sometimes becomes essential.

Online dating and security

If a person stays safe, the internet may be a fantastic way to build connections.

People should keep in mind the following guidelines while using the internet:

Nobody is obligated to share or upload anything they want not to.

If someone chooses to follow up an online encounter with a physical one, they should take measures.

Assume that everyone can access any material posted online.

Never give out any personal information to anybody online, including your entire name, address, and date of birth.

Never watch any sexually explicit videos that include children under the age of 18.

Using sexual expression

Sexual desires are normal human emotions that are not to be shunned. It is also normal for someone to not feel sexually attracted to anybody. Never should a person be forced to feel guilty about their sexual orientation.

An autistic person may benefit from expressing their sexuality. There is a connection between sexual dissatisfaction, depressive symptoms, and worse mental health, according to research by 2020Trusted Source. Sexual practices may make an autistic person feel less stressed or anxious.

The challenges of sexual activity may increase due to several elements of autism. An autistic person may, however, discuss any issues or concerns they may have with their spouse or other close family members.

It might be crucial to assist autistic people in comprehending their sexual sensations and navigating a variety of connected challenges. People may feel uneasy or unprepared when it comes to sex if they lack sufficient information.

Printed in Great Britain
by Amazon

17642434R00047